CONTENT

Before you start 5

EVERYDAY OBJECTS

ALARM CLOCK 7
BACKPACK 16
BALL 6
BALLOON 13
BATHTUB 19
BOOK 16
BOTTLE 18
BRUSH 7
BUCKET 6
CAMERA 12
CHAIR 18
CLOCK 11
COFFEE TABLE 19
CUP 18
DOOR 9
DRONE 12
ERASER 17
FAN 7
GLASSES 11

GUITAR 15
HAT 13
HIGH HEEL SHOES 10
HOUSE 9
KEYS 9
LAMP 16
LAPTOP 8
MAGNIFYING GLASS 8
MICROPHONE 15
MIRROR 14
NOTEBOOK 17
PENCIL 17
PENCIL SHARPENER 17
PHONE 11
PILLOW 13
REFRIGERATOR 19
ROPE 6
RULER 6
SANDALS 10

SCISSORS 13
SHOES 10
SHOPPING BAG 14
SHOPPING CART 14
SPEAKER 15
TABLE 18
THERMOMETER 8
THREAD 14
TOOTHBRUSH 10
TOWELS 19
TV 11
UMBRELLA 16
VASE 8
VIDEO GAME CONSOLE 12
VIDEO GAME CONTROLLER 12
VIOLIN 15
WALL CLOCK 7
WINDOW 9

FOOD

APPLE 20
AVOCADO 31
BANANA 20
BELL PEPPER 30
BIRTHDAY CAKE 28

BREAD 25
BROCCOLI 24
BURRITO 26
CAKE 22
CANDY 26

CARROT 21
CEREAL 32
CHEESE 29
CHERRY 29
CHOCOLATE 32

COCONUT 30
COFFEE MAKER 25
COOKIE 22
CROISSANT 27
CUPCAKE 28
DONUT 21
DOUBLE BURGER 31
DOUBLE ICE CREAM 31
FORTUNE COOKIE 25
FRENCH FRIES 27
FRIED EGG 29
GRAPES 23

HAMBURGER 23
HOT DOG 21
ICE CREAM 31
JUICE 32
LEMON 24
LOLLIPOP 25
MILK 32
MORE SUSHI 27
PEACH 24
PINEAPPLE 28
PIZZA 20
POPCORN 23

POPSICLE 23
SALAD 26
SANDWICH 22
SLICE OF PIZZA 20
SODA 28
SPAGHETTI 29
STRAWBERRY 21
SUSHI 27
TACO 26
TOMATO 30
WATERMELON 22
YOGURT 24
ZUCCHINI 30

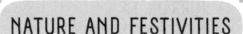

NATURE AND FESTIVITIES

AUTUMN LEAVES 37
CACTUS 36
CANDLE 44
CAVE 40
CHRISTMAS BERRY 43
CHRISTMAS STAR 42
CHRISTMAS STOCKINGS 42
CHRISTMAS TREE 41
CLIFF 38
CLOUD
CONFETTI 45
CORNFIELD 39
DESERT 38
DOVE OF PEACE 43
EASTER BUNNY PAW 44
EASTER EGG 44
FALLING SNOW 40
FIELD OF FLOWERS 36
FIREWORKS 45

FLOWER 37
FOREST 36
GARDEN FENCE
GRADUATION HAT 45
GRASS 34
HEART (VALENTINE'S DAY) 45
HILLS LANDSCAPE 38
LIGHTHOUSE 38
LIGHTNING 39
MOON
MOUNTAIN
MUSHROOM 37
PALM 37
PARTY HAT 44
POINSETTIA 43
RAINBOW
RAINDROPS 39
REINDEER 41
RIVER 35

SANTA CLAUS 41
SEA COAST
SHOOTING STAR 36
SNOW 40
SNOW-COVERED HILLS 41
SNOWMAN 42
STALACTITES 40
STAR
SUN 33
TREE
WATERFALL
WIND (WAVY LINES) 39
WITCH BROOM 46
WITCH CAULDRON 46
WITCH HAT 46
WITCH WAND 46
WRAPPED GIFT 43
WREATH 42

TRANSPORTATION MEANS

AIRPLANE 48
AMBULANCE 52
BICYCLE 47
BLIMP 52
BOAT 48
BUS 51
CAR FRONT VIEW 47
CAR SIDE VIEW 47
DOUBLE-DECKER BUS 53
FIRE TRUCK 52
HELICOPTER 49
HOT AIR BALLOON 55

HOVERCRAFT 54
LIMOUSINE 53
MOTOCROSS 54
MOTORCYCLE 50
OLD MOTORCYCLE 53
POLICE CAR 54
RACE CAR 51
ROWBOAT 51
SAILBOAT 54
SCHOOL BUS 49
SCOOTER 50
SKATEBOARD 55

SLED 55
SPACESHIP 49
SPEEDBOAT 53
SUBMARINE 49
TAXI 51
TRACTOR 50
TRAIN 48
TRAM 55
TRUCK 48
VAN 47
YACHT 52

ANIMALS

ANT 72
BAT 69
BEAR 56
BEAR PAW PRINTS 56
BEAVER 60
BEE 66
BIRD 64
BUTTERFLY 58
CAMEL 70
CAT 62
CHICK 59
CORAL 57
COW 71
CRAB 71
DOG 62
DOLPHIN 56
DUCK 63
ELEPHANT 68
FISH 64
FLAMINGO 65

FOX 70
FROG 71
GIRAFFE 67
HEDGEHOG 66
HEN 59
HIPPOPOTAMUS 73
IGUANA 69
JELLYFISH 60
KANGAROO 63
KITTEN 61
KOALA 63
LADYBUG 72
LION 68
LLAMA 59
MANTA RAY 57
MONKEY 75
MOOSE 60
OCTOPUS 69
OYSTER 59

OWL 65
PARROT 70
PENGUIN 69
PIG 65
PUFFER FISH 57
PUPPY 61
RABBIT 58
RHINOCEROS 74
SEAHORSE 65
SEAL 60
SHARK 67
SNAIL 63
SNAKE 66
SQUIRREL 73
TIGER 75
TURTLE 56
WALRUS 72
WHALE 57
ZEBRA 74

PEOPLE, SPORTS AND HOBBIES

Different ways to draw eyes, mouths, etc. 76
Facial Expressions 78

ANCHOR 102
ASTRONAUT 89
ASTRONAUT IN SPACE 91
BASKETBALL HOOP AND BALL 98
BASKETBALL PLAYER 98
BISHOP CHESS PIECE 105
BOWLING ALLEY 104
BOWLING BALL 104
BOWLING PINS 104
CAP 102
CASTLE 94
CHECKERS 107
CHEF 82
CHEF HAT 82
CHESS BOARD 106
CHESS CLOCK 106
CLIMBING ROPE 96
CROWN 92
DENTIST 83
DENTIST CHAIR AND LIGHT 83
DICE 107
DISH 82
DIVING FINS 103
DOMINOES 107
DRAGON 95
DRAGON EYE 95
EARTH 90
EXTINGUISHER 86
FAIRY TALE CASTLE 94
FIRE FLAME 96
FIREFIGHTER 85
FIREFIGHTER 86

FIREFIGHTER BADGE 85
FIREFIGHTER HELMET 85
FLOATY 102
FLYING SAUCER 89
FRISBEE 103
HAWAIIAN SHIRT 101
HYDRANT 86
JUMP ROPE 108
JUPITER 90
KING CHESS PIECE 106
KITE 101
KNIGHT 105
MAGIC MIRROW 94
MEDICINE 81
MEDIEVAL KNIGHT 95
METEORITE 90
MICROSCOPE AND LAB FLASK 80
NINJA 96
NURSE 81
PAPER PLANE 87
PAWN CHESS PIECE 105
PENCILS INSIDE A JAR 87
PILOT 88
PILOT HAT 88
PIRATE 97
PIRATE MAP 97
PIRATE SCARF 97
PLANET WITH CRATERS 90
PLAYING CARDS 107
POLICE BADGE 84
POLICE CAP 84
POLICE OFFICER 84
POOL 108

PRINCESS 92
PRINCESS HAT 95
QUEEN 93
QUEEN CHESS PIECE 106
ROBOT 109
ROBOT WAVING 109
ROBOTIC ARM 109
ROOK CHESS PIECE 105
RUGBY BALL 103
SAND BUCKET 102
SATELLITE 89
SCEPTER 93
SCIENTIST 80
SOCCER BALL 99
SOCCER GOAL 99
SOCCER PLAYER 99
SPIRAL GALAXY 91
SPIRAL GALAXY 91
STETHOSCOPE 81
SUPERHERO 110
SUPERHERO MASK 110
SURFBOARD 101
SURVEILLANCE ROBOT 109
TEACHER 87
TEDDY BEAR 108
TENNIS BALL 100
TENNIS COURT 100
TENNIS RACKET 100
THRONE 93
TIARA 92
TRAMPOLINE 108

Before you start

YOUR GIFT

Here are some easy instructions to help you learn to draw!

1 Grab your sharp pencil and your favorite eraser.

2 The grey circles or ovals are just to help you. Start by tracing them very lightly.

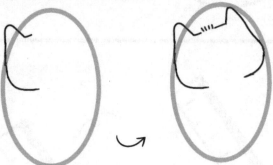

3 When drawing, use gentle lines to make a neat outline and fix mistakes easily.

4 Follow each drawing diagram step by step.

5 If you want to add a dash color to your creation, colored pencils are your best choice.

Make sure to start from the first pages of the book and move forward, as the drawings get harder little by little.

In this book, you'll find drawings in various styles and learn lots of cool tricks! With "Objects," you'll learn how to draw things and add 3D shading. With "Landscapes," you'll practice making thin and thick lines. "Vehicles" will be a fun challenge for drawing straight lines. And with "Characters," you'll learn how to draw people with different facial expressions.

It's not about drawing things perfectly; it's about having fun!

BALL

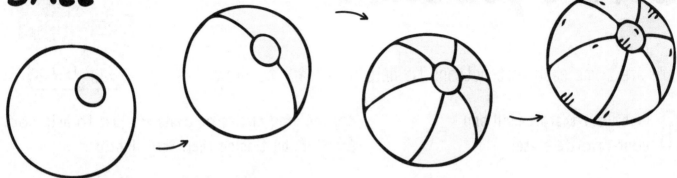

RULER

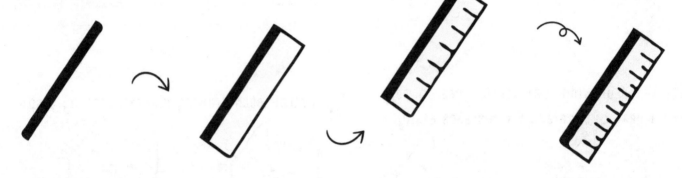

BUCKET

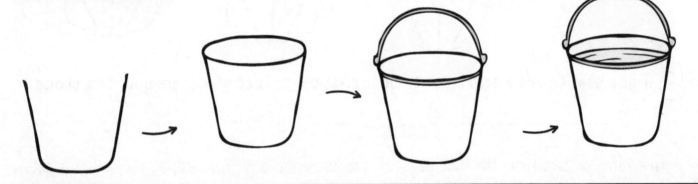

ROPE

FAN

ALARM

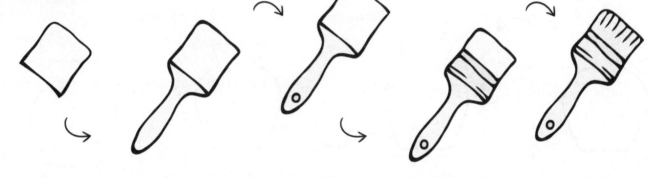

BRUSH

WALL CLOCK

LAPTOP

THERMOMETER

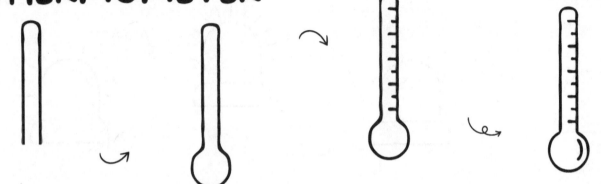

VASE

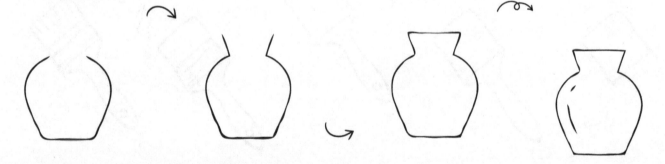

MAGNIFYING GLASS

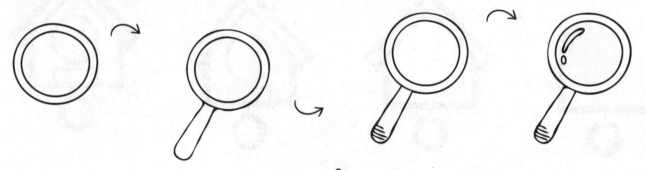

HOUSE

WINDOW

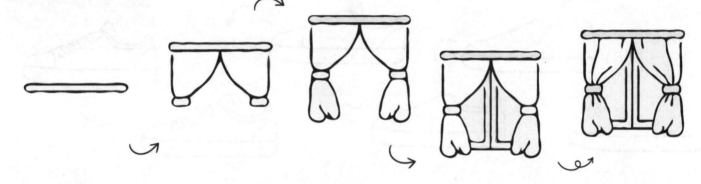

DOOR

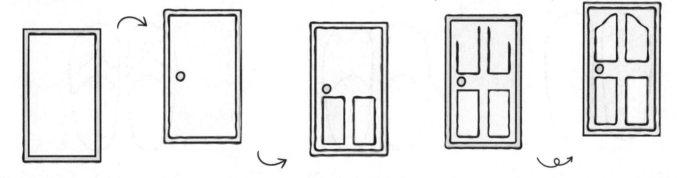

KEYS

9

TOOTHBRUSH

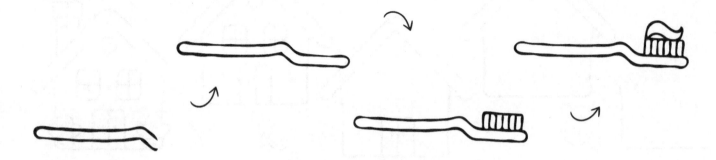

SHOES

SANDALS

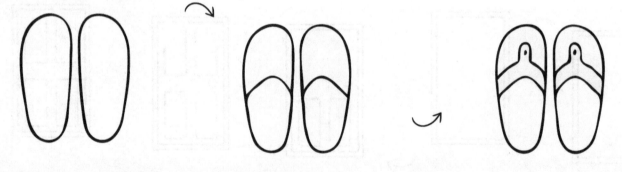

HIGH HEEL SHOES

CLOCK

TV

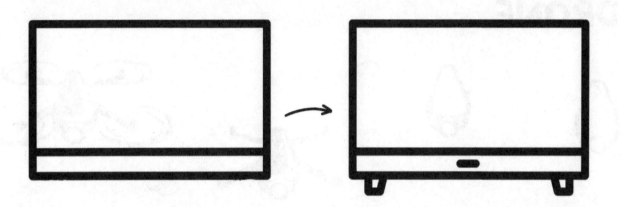

PHONE

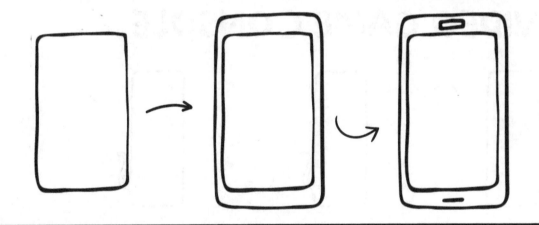

GLASSES

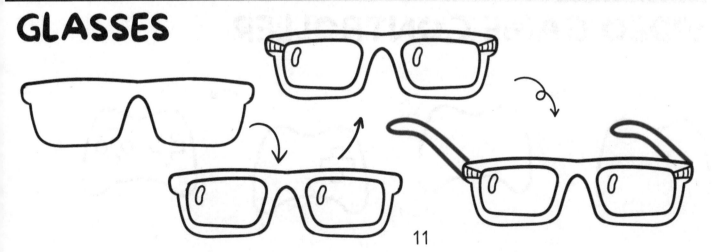

11

CAMERA

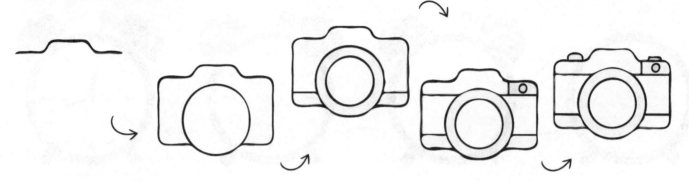

DRONE

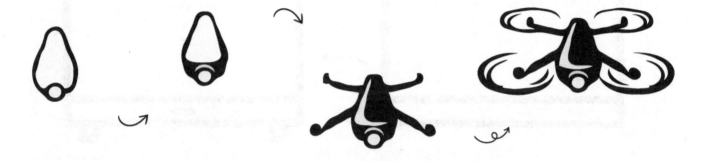

VIDEO GAME CONSOLE

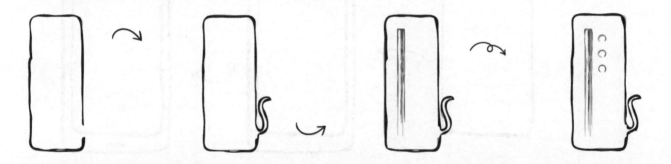

VIDEO GAME CONTROLLER

PILLOW

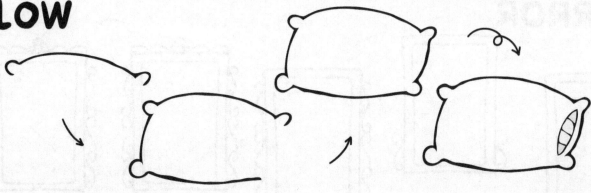

SCISSORS

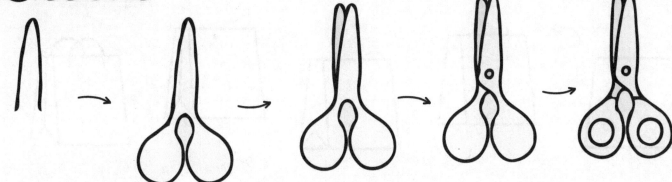

BALLOON

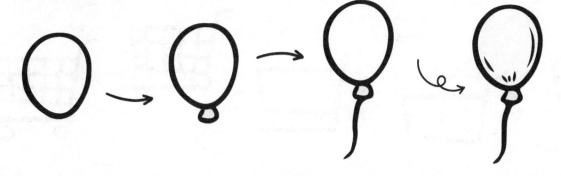

HAT

MIRROR

SHOPPING BAG

SHOPPING CART

THREAD

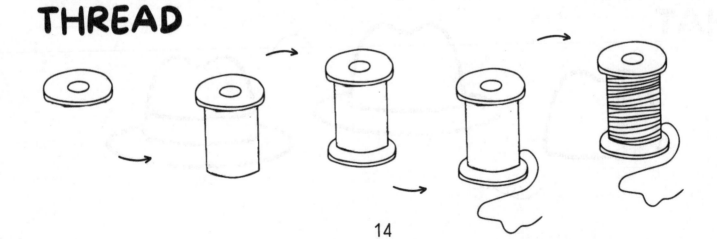

GUITAR

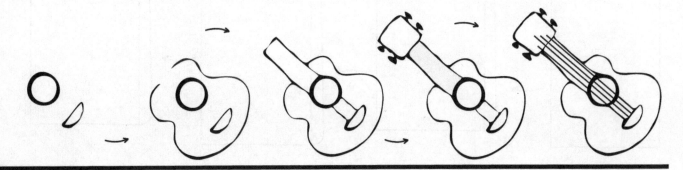

VIOLIN

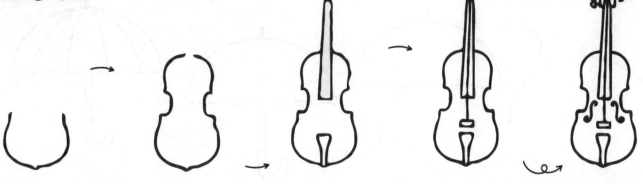

SPEAKER

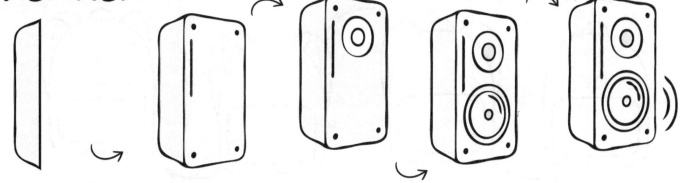

MICROPHONE

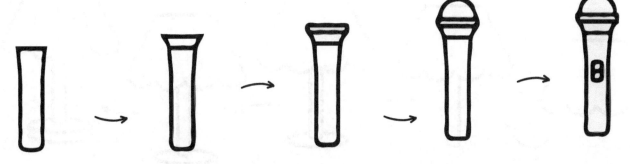

BOOK

UMBRELLA

BACKPACK

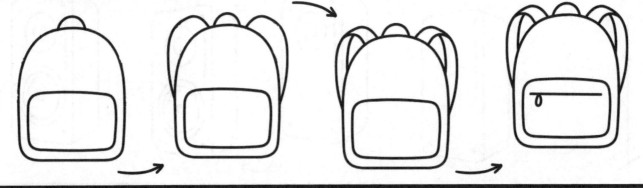

LAMP

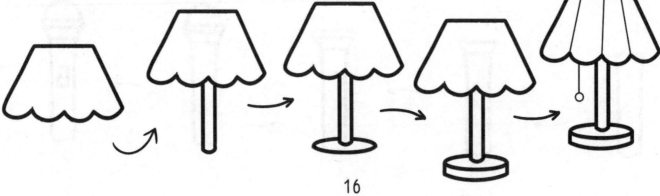

16

PENCIL

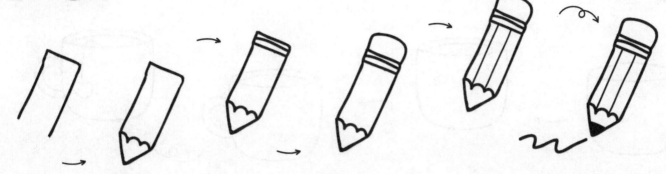

ERASER

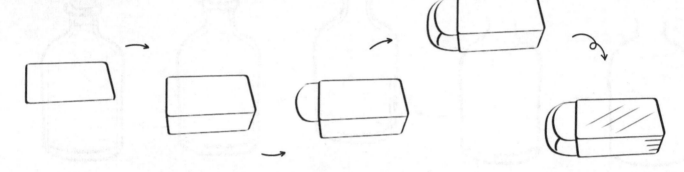

PENCIL SHARPENER

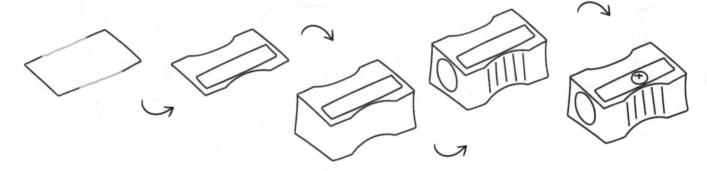

NOTEBOOK

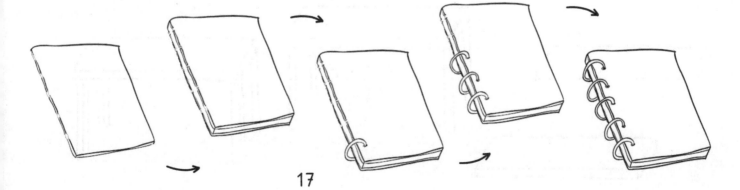

CUP

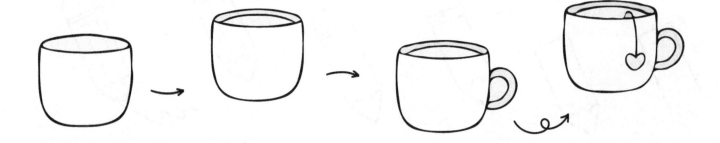

BOTTLE

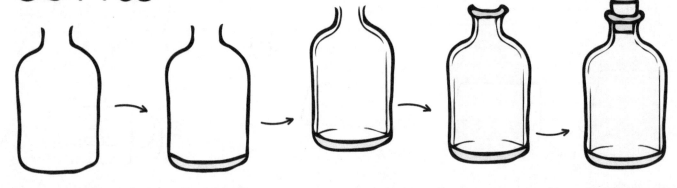

CHAIR

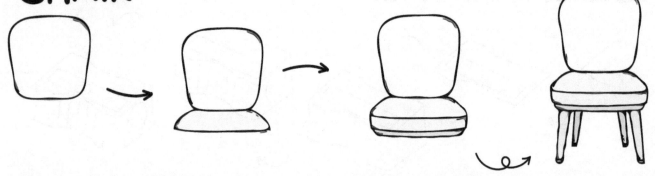

TABLE

REFRIGERATOR

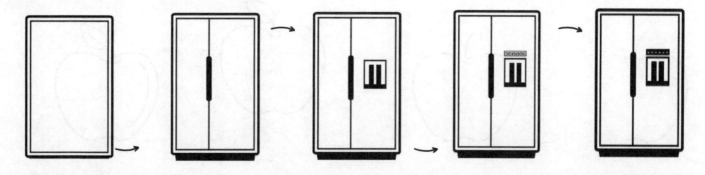

TOWELS

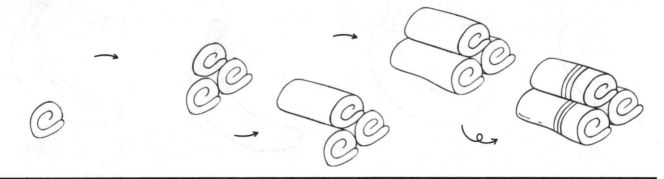

BATHTUB

COFFEE TABLE

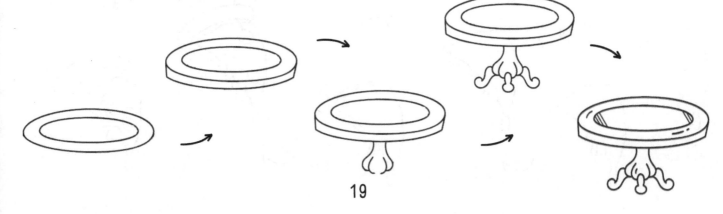

APPLE

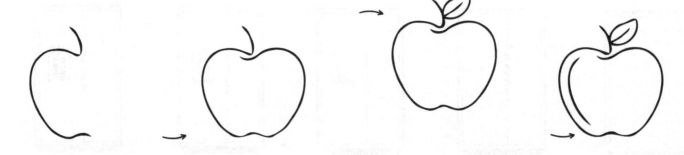

BANANA

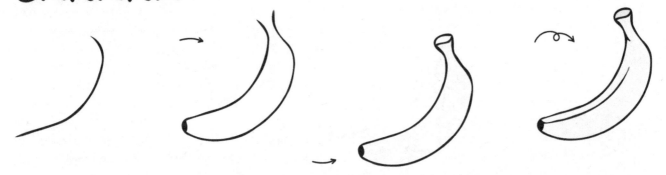

PIZZA

SLICE OF PIZZA

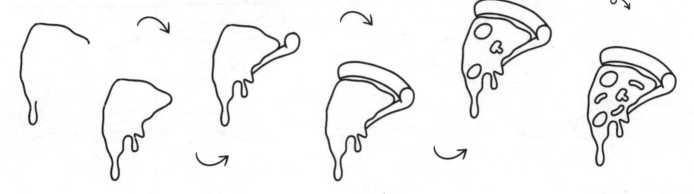

CARROT

DONUT

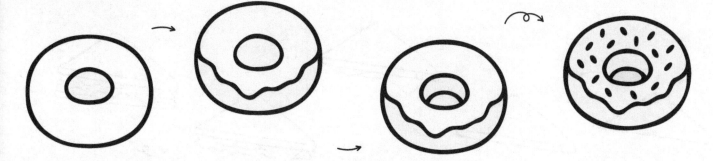

STRAWBERRY

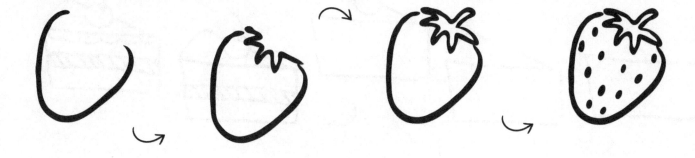

HOT DOG

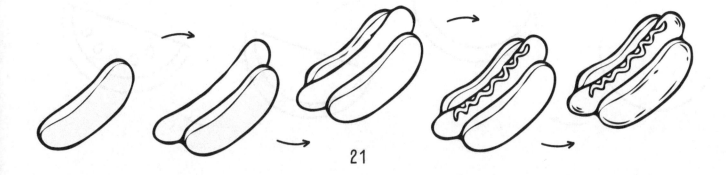

21

COOKIE

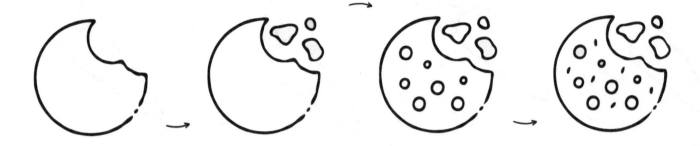

SANDWICH

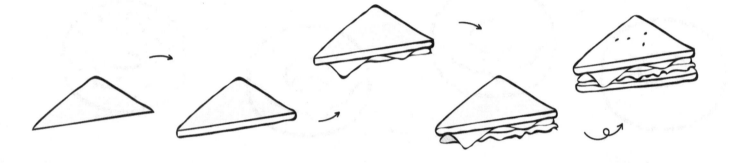

CAKE

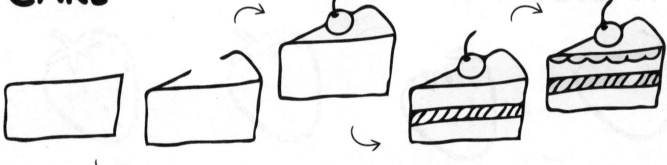

WATERMELON

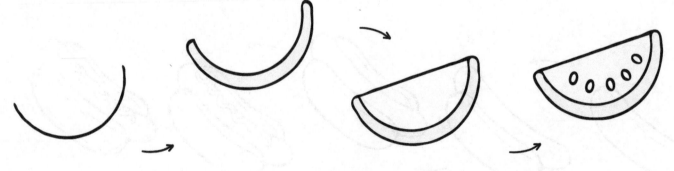

POPSICLE

HAMBURGER

GRAPES

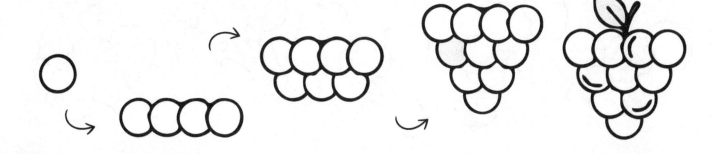

POPCORN

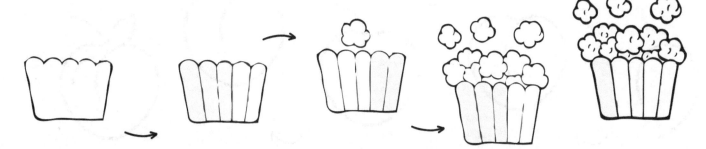

LEMON

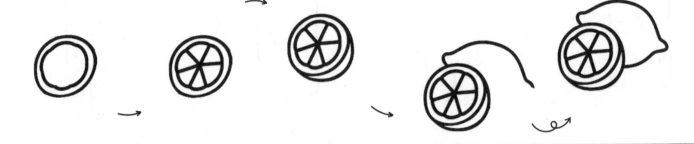

YOGURT

BROCCOLI

PEACH

24

LOLLIPOP

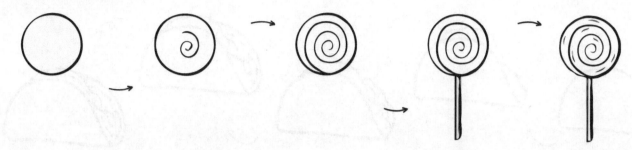

COFFEE MAKER

BREAD

FORTUNE COOKIE

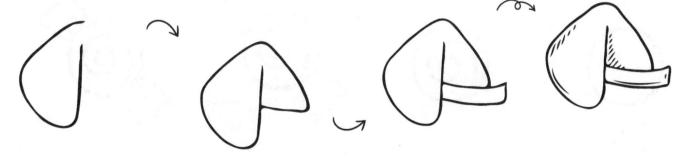

TACO

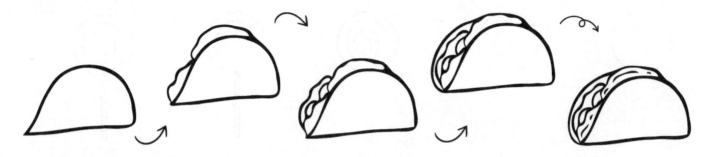

BURRITO

SALAD

CANDY

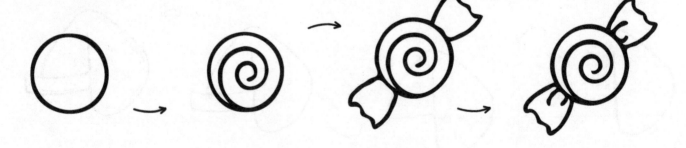

FRENCH FRIES

SUSHI

MORE SUSHI

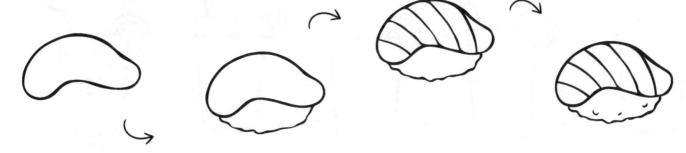

CROISSANT

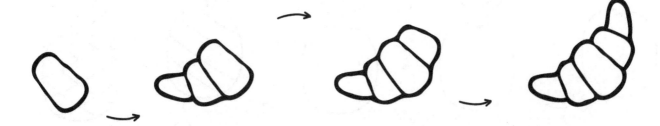

BIRTHDAY CAKE

CUPCAKE

SODA

PINEAPPLE

CHERRY

SPAGHETTI

CHEESE

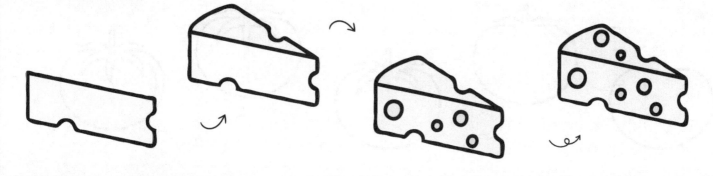

FRIED EGG

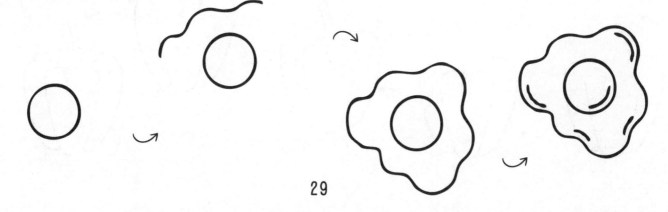

ZUCCHINI

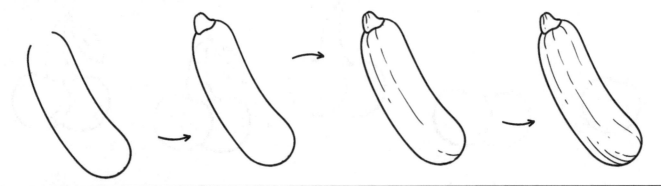

COCONUT

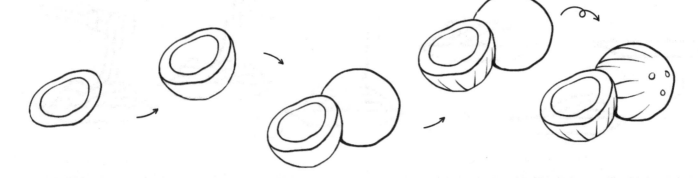

TOMATO

BELL PEPPER

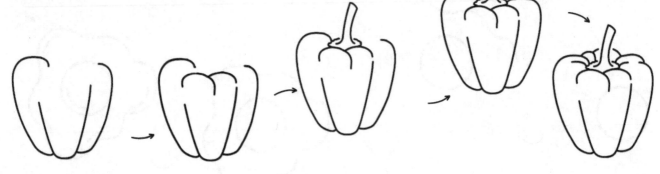

AVOCADO

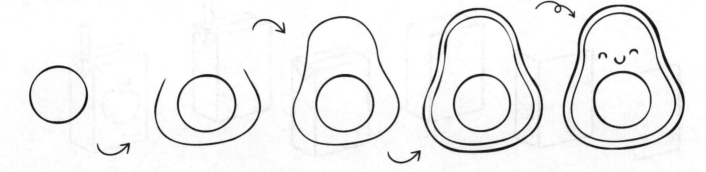

DOUBLE BURGER

ICE CREAM

BIG ICE CREAM

JUICE

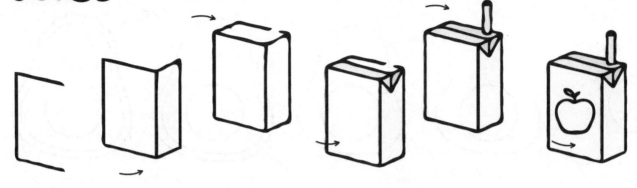

MILK

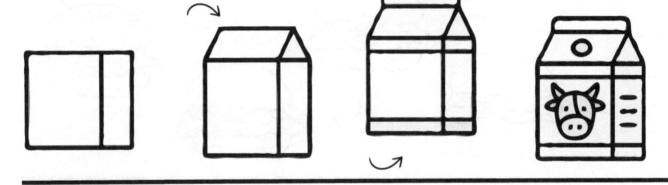

CEREAL

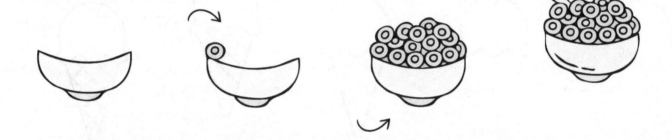

CHOCOLATE

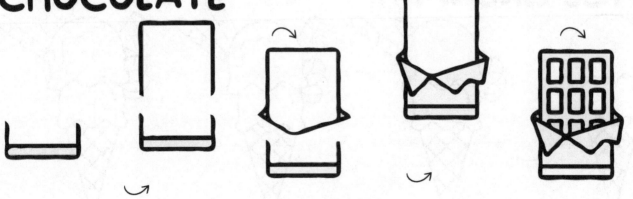

SUN

CLOUD

TREE

MOUNTAIN

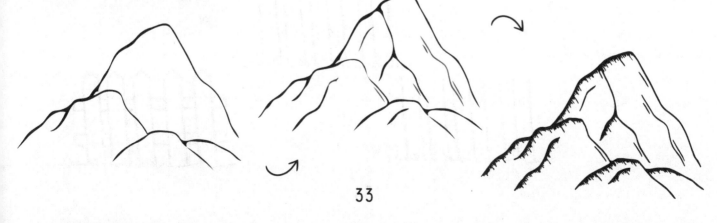

GRASS

SEA COAST

WATERFALL

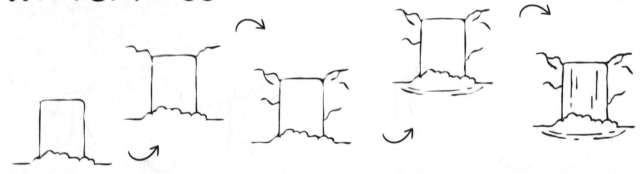

GARDEN FENCE

RIVER

MOON

RAINBOW

STAR

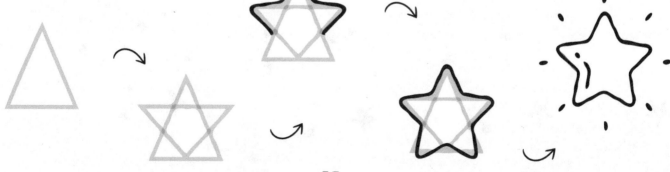

FOREST

FIELD OF FLOWERS

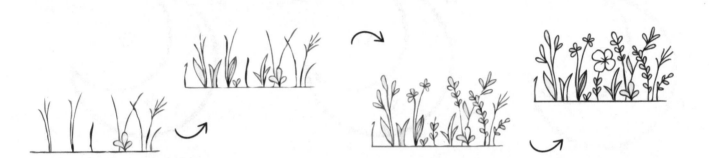

CACTUS

SHOOTING STAR

FLOWER

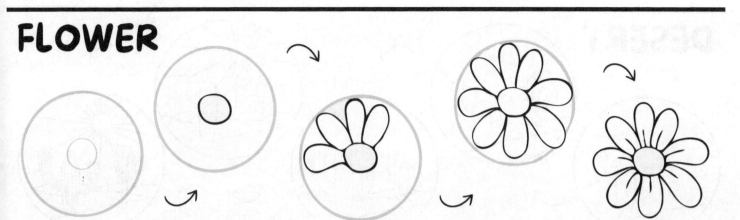

PALM

AUTUMN LEAVES

MUSHROOM

DESERT

LIGHTHOUSE

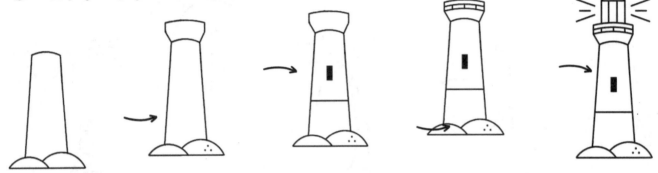

CLIFT

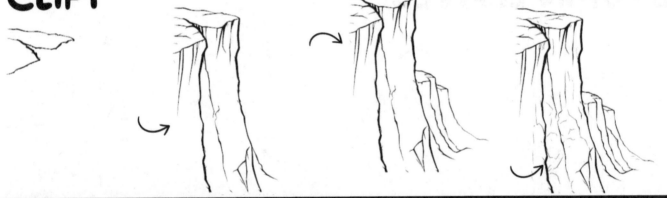

HILLS LANDSCAPE

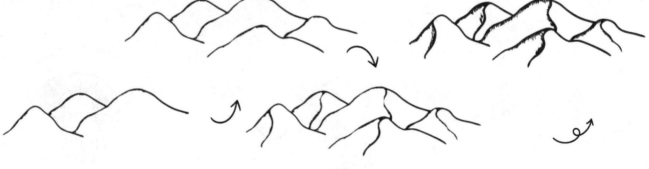

CORNFIELD

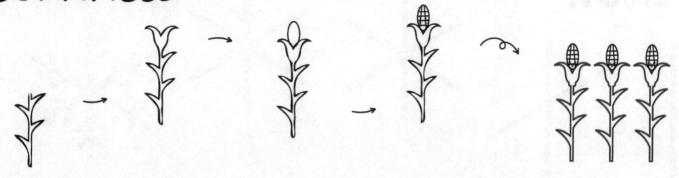

WIND (WAVY LINES)

RAINDROPS

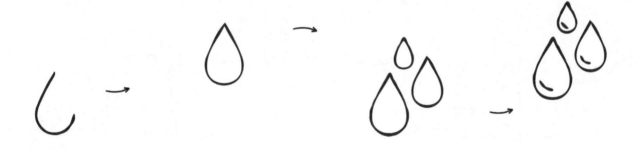

LIGHTNING

SNOW

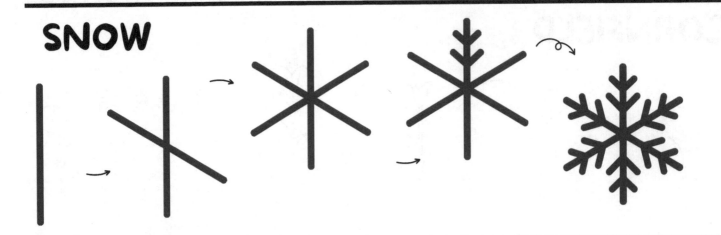

FALLING SNOW

CAVE

STALACTITES

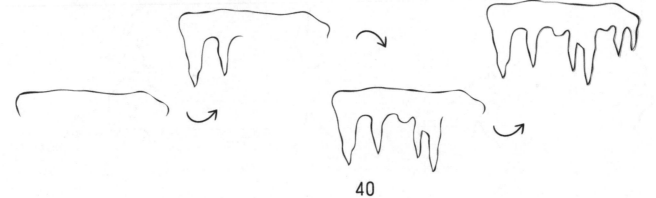

SNOW-COVERED HILLS

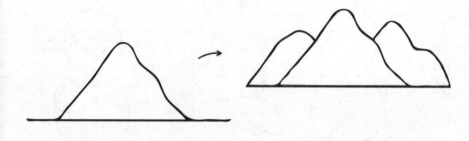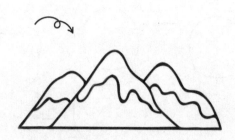

SANTA CLAUS

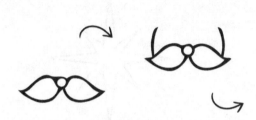

REINDEER

CHRISTMAS TREE

SNOWMAN

CHRISTMAS STAR

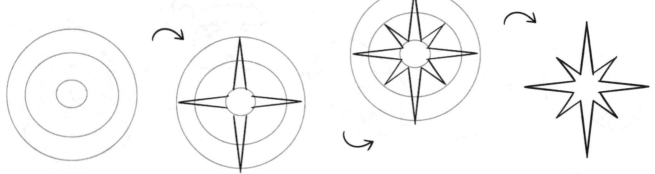

CHRISTMAS STOCKINGS

WREATH

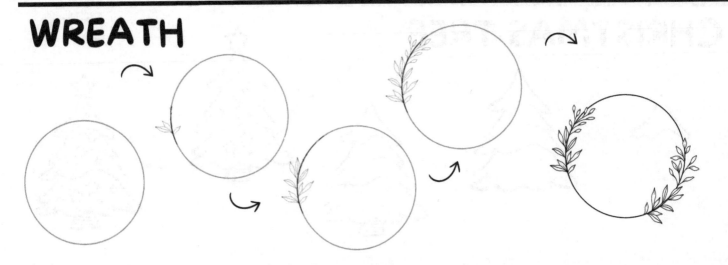

POINSETTIA

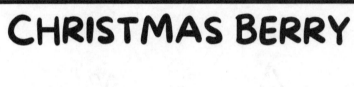

CHRISTMAS BERRY

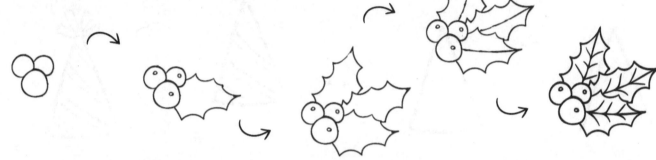

WRAPPED GIFT

DOVE OF PEACE

CANDLE

PARTY HAT

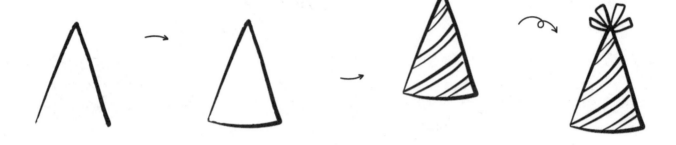

EASTER EGG

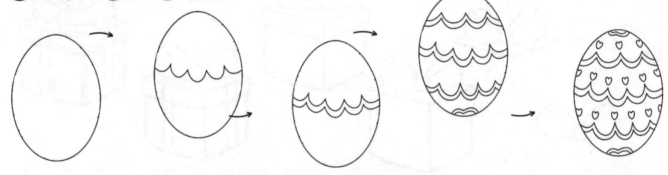

EASTER BUNNY PAW

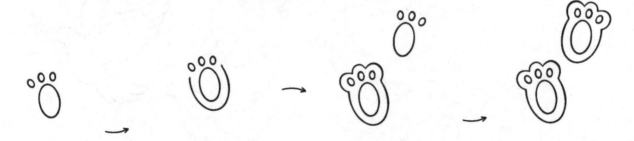

44

HEART (VALENTINE'S DAY)

FIREWORKS

CONFETTI

GRADUATION HAT

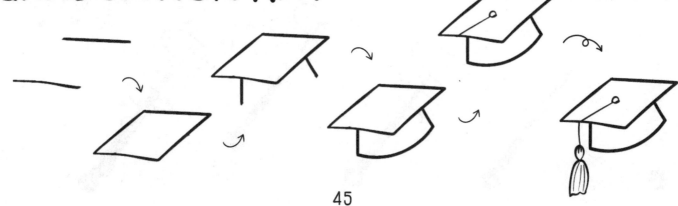

WITCH BROOM

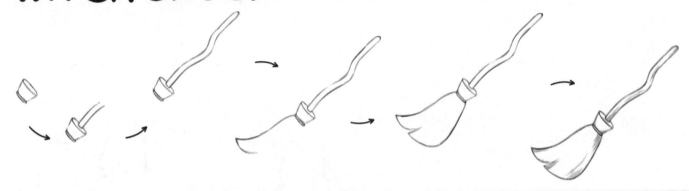

WITCH CAULDRON

WITCH HAT

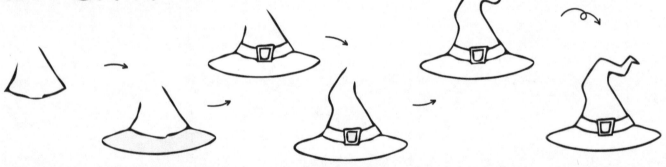

WITCH WAND

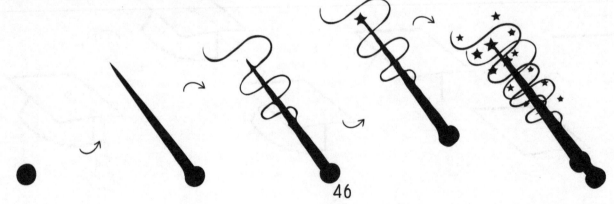

CAR SIDE VIEW

CAR FRONT VIEW

VAN

BICYCLE

TRAIN

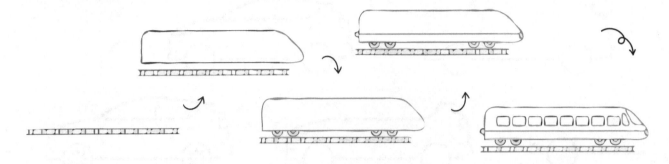

BOAT

AIRPLANE

TRUCK

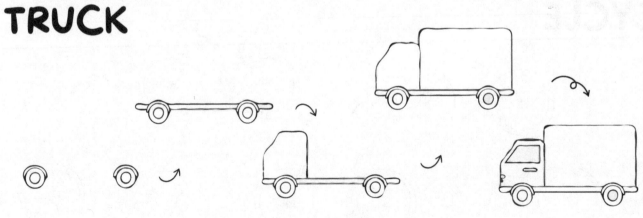

SCHOOL BUS

SPACESHIP

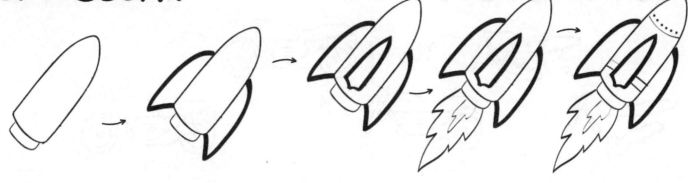

HELICOPTER

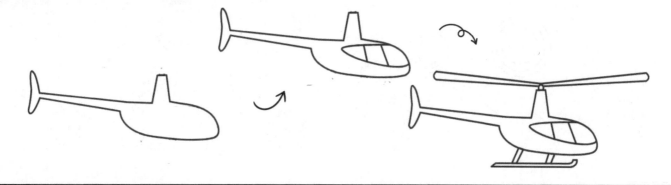

SUBMARINE

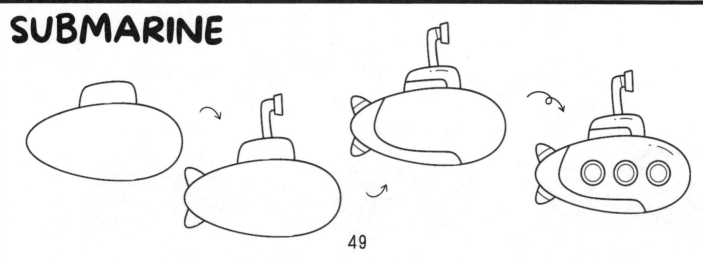

49

SCOOTER

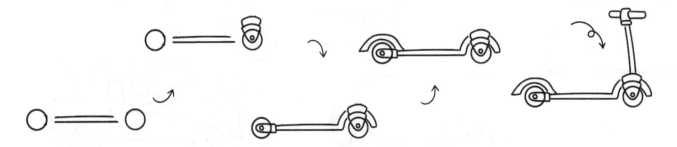

MOTORCYCLE

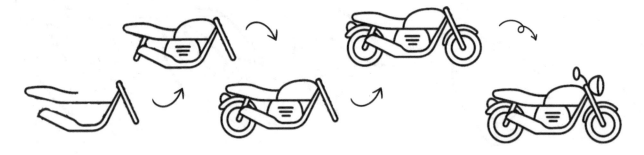

TRACTOR

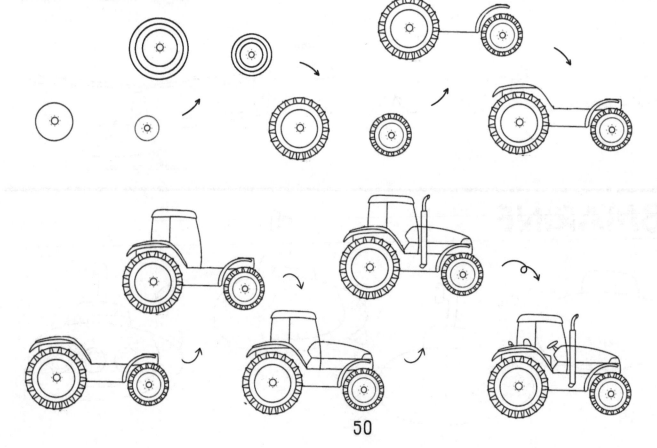

50

ROWBOAT

TAXI

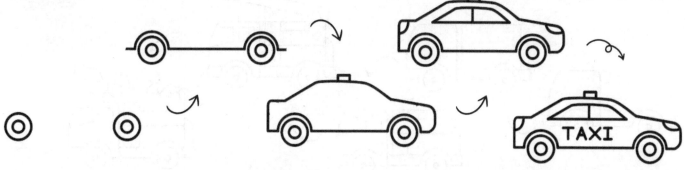

BUS

RACE CAR

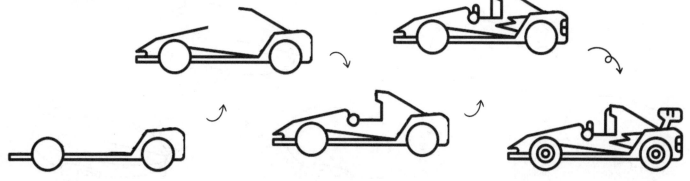

YACHT

FIRE TRUCK

AMBULANCE

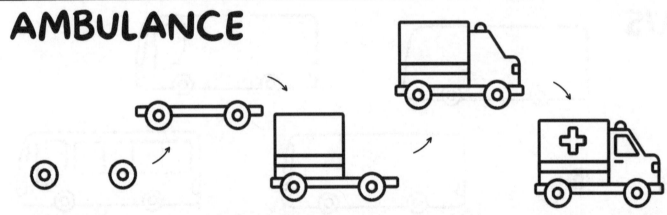

BLIMP

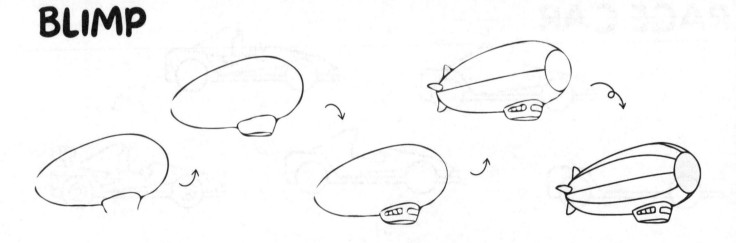

LIMOUSINE

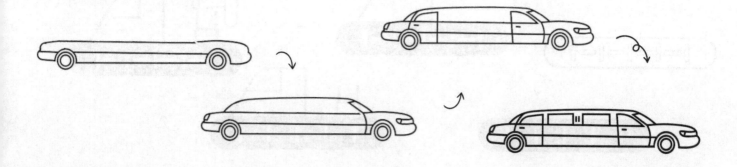

DOUBLE-DECKER BUS

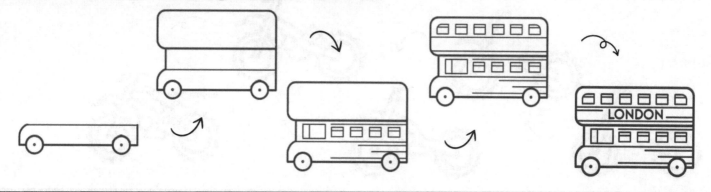

OLD MOTORCYCLE

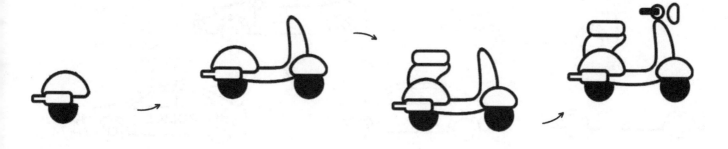

SPEEDBOAT

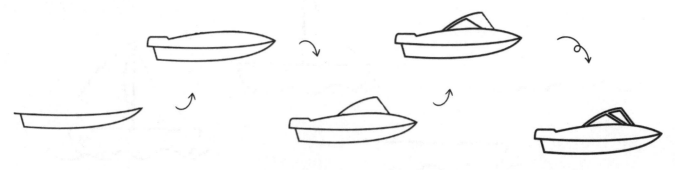

HOVERCRAFT

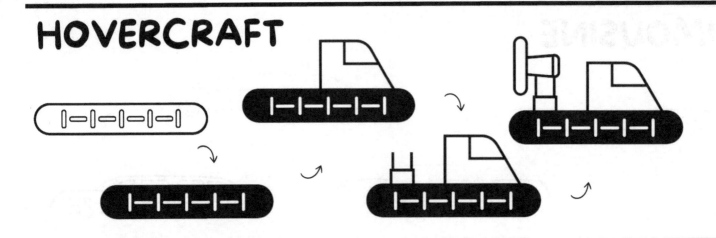

MOTOCROSS

POLICE CAR

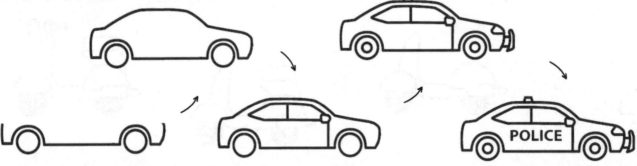

SAILBOAT

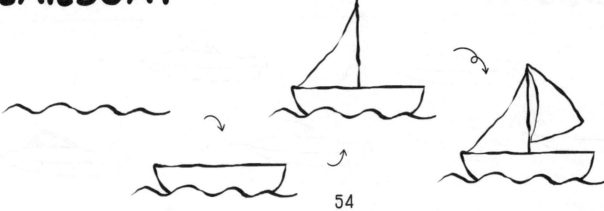

TRAM

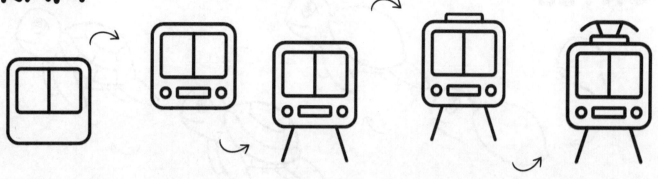

SKATEBOARD

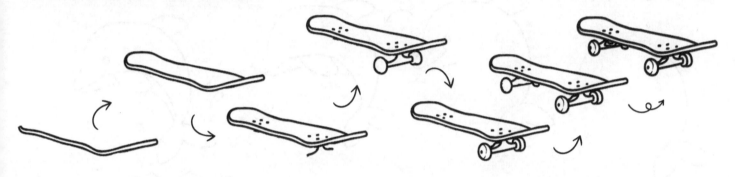

SLED

HOT AIR BALLOON

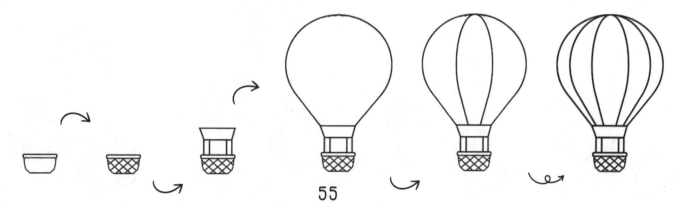

TURTLE

DOLPHIN

BEAR

BEAR PAW PRINTS

WHALE

MANTA RAY

PUFFER FISH

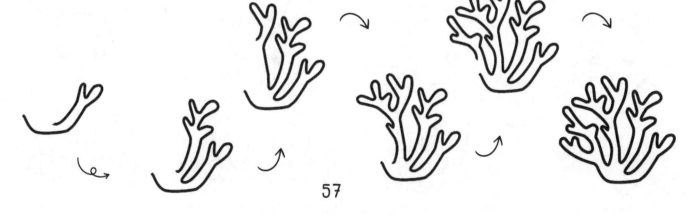

CORAL

BUTTERFLY

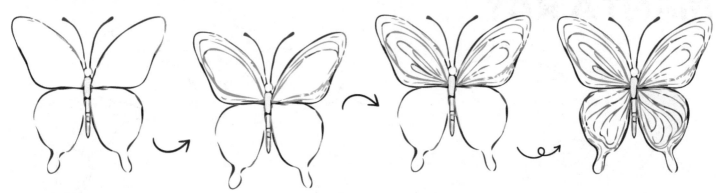

RABBIT

58

HEN

CHICK

LLAMA

OYSTER

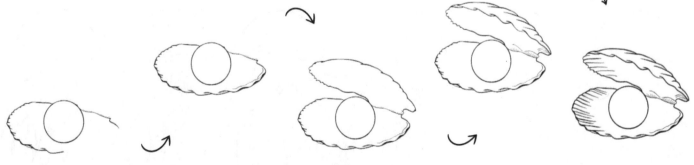

SEAL

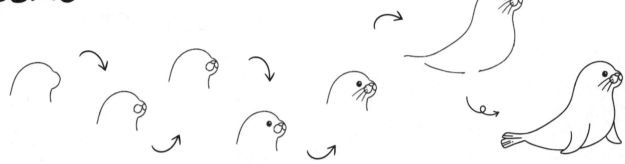

BEAVER

MOOSE

JELLYFISH

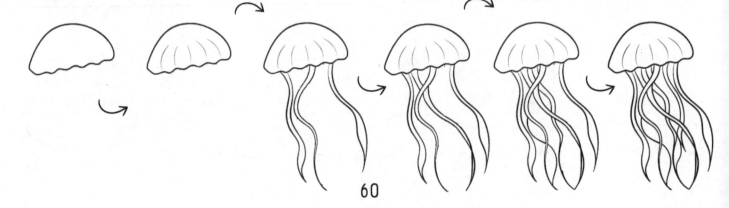

KITTEN

PUPPY

CAT

DOG

DUCK

SNAIL

KOALA

KANGAROO

63

FISH

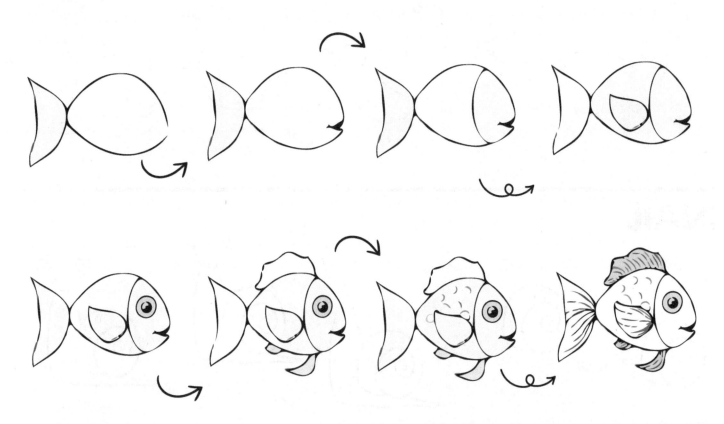

BIRD

OWL

SEAHORSE

FLAMINGO

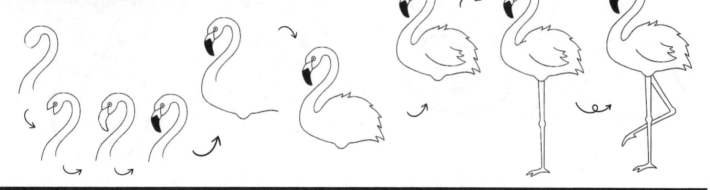

PIG

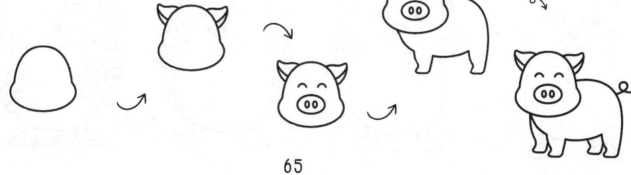

65

SNAKE

BEE

HEDGEHOG

GIRAFFE

SHARK

ELEPHANT

LION

OCTOPUS

PENGUIN

IGUANA

BAT

PARROT

CAMEL

FOX

COW

CRAB

FROG

WALRUS

LADYBUG

ANT

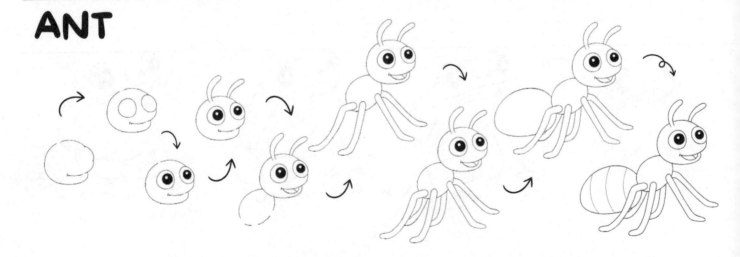

HIPPOPOTAMUS

SQUIRREL

ZEBRA

RHINOCEROS

TIGER

MONKEY

75

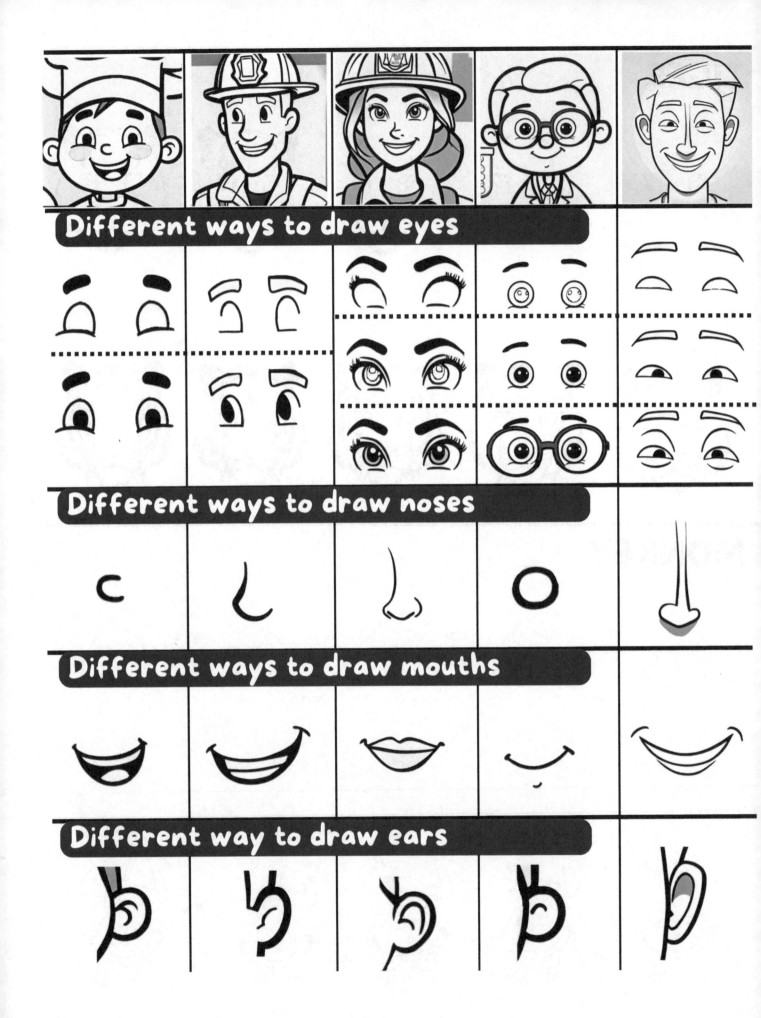

Different ways to draw eyes

Different ways to draw noses

Different ways to draw mouths

Different way to draw ears

Now it's your turn; try different combinations of mouths, noses, ears, and eyes!

FACIAL EXPRESSIONS

You can express different emotions just by changing the position of your eyebrows and mouth. Grab a mirror and see for yourself!

neutral face

malicious face

same eyebrows different mouth

sad face

different eyebrows same mouth

angry face

happy face

different eyebrows same mouth

shame face

Your turn! Try creating different expressions by changing the eyebrows and mouth on the blank faces in the book. How many can you come up with?

SCIENTIST

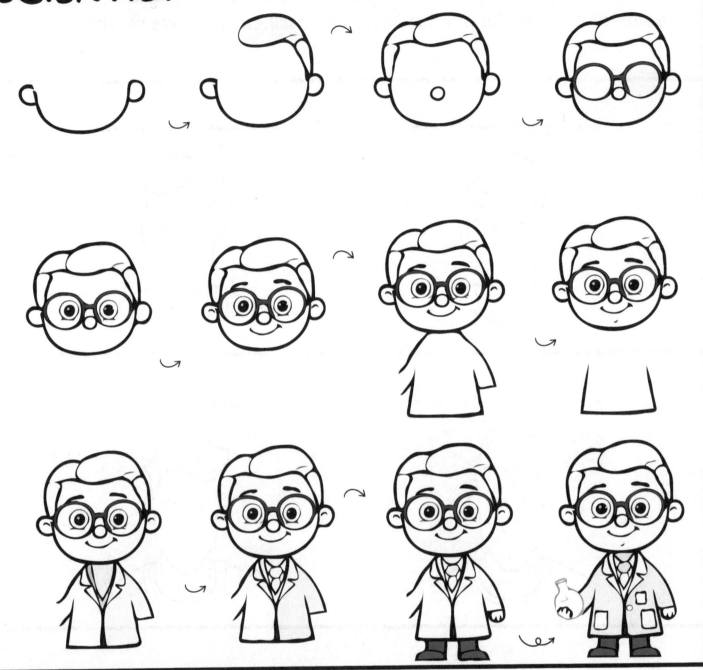

MICROSCOPE AND LAB FLASK

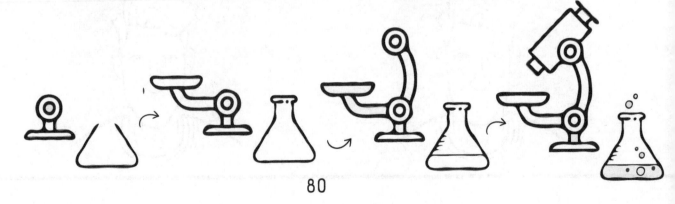

80

NURSE

MEDICINE AND STETHOSCOPE

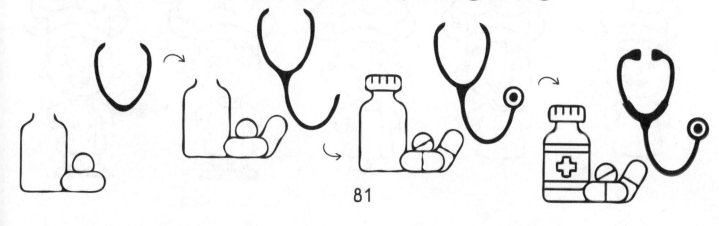

81

DISH

CHEF HAT

CHEF

DENTIST

DENTIST CHAIR AND LIGHT

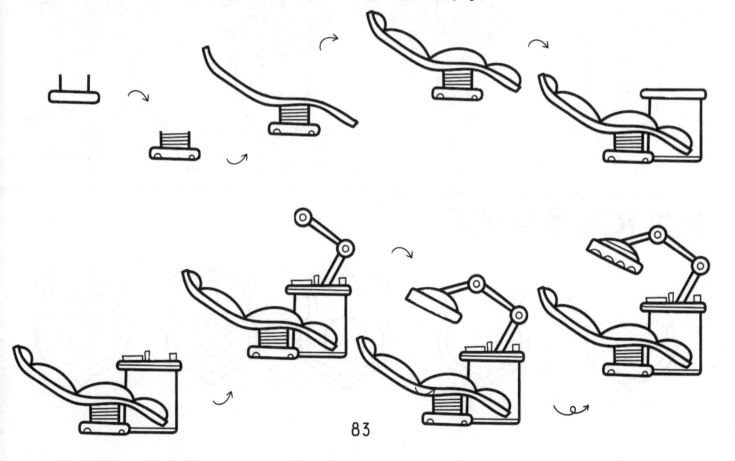

83

POLICE CAP

POLICE OFFICER

POLICE BADGE

FIREFIGHTER HELMET

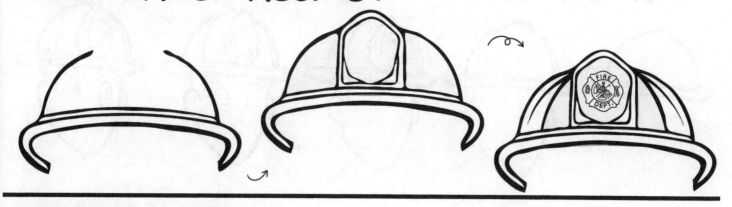

FIREFIGHTER

FIREFIGHTER BADGE

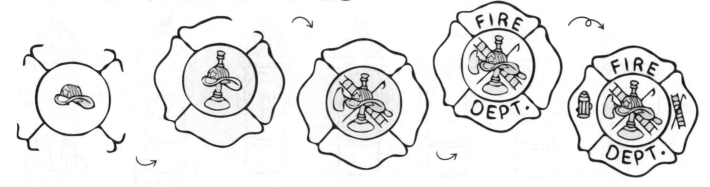

FIREFIGHTER

EXTINGUISHER

HYDRANT

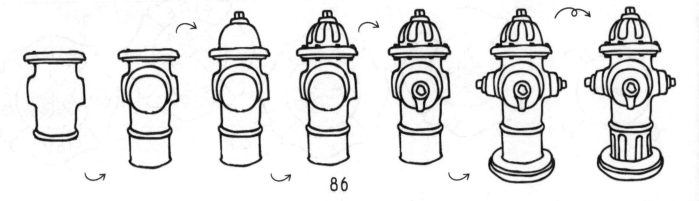

TEACHER

PENCILS INSIDE A JAR

PAPER PLANE

PILOT HAT

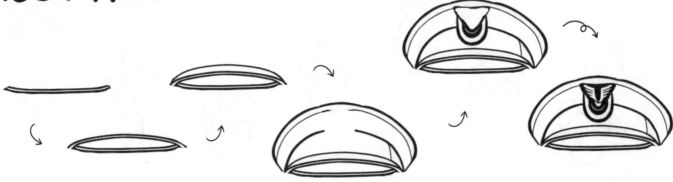

PILOT

WINGS

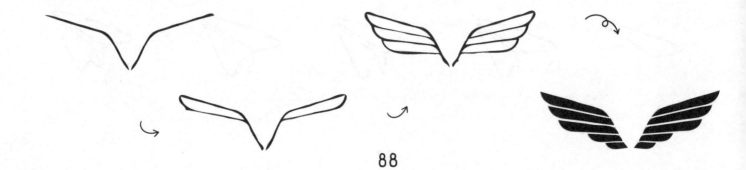

88

ASTRONAUT

SATELLITE

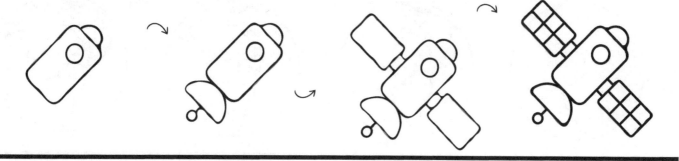

FLYING SAUCER

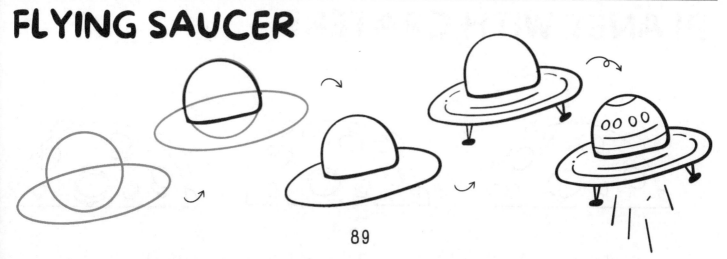

METEORITE

JUPITER

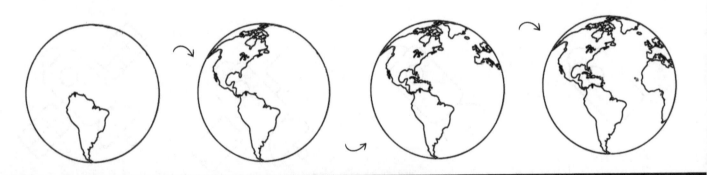

EARTH

PLANET WITH CRATERS

SPIRAL GALAXY

ASTRONAUT IN SPACE

SPACE STATION

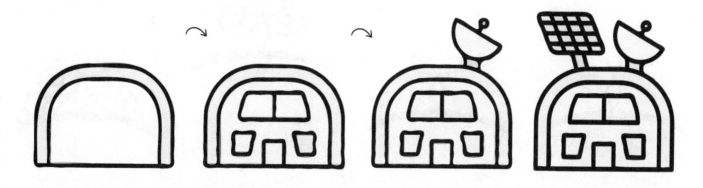

PRINCESS

CROWN

TIARA

QUEEN

THRONE

SCEPTER

CASTLE

MAGIC MIRROW

FAIRY TALE CASTLE

94

MEDIEVAL KNIGHT

PRINCESS HAT

DRAGON

DRAGON EYE

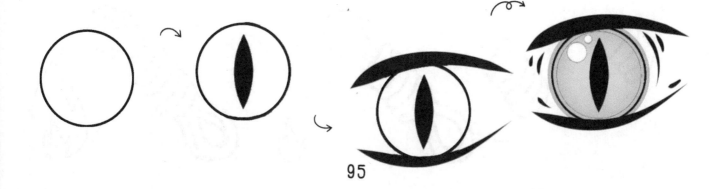

NINJA

CLIMBING ROPE AND FIRE FLAME

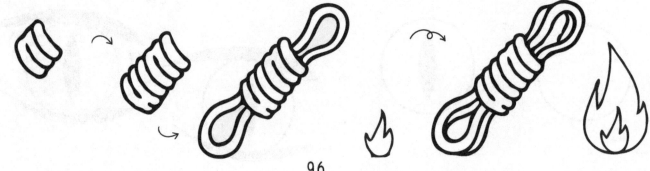

PIRATE MAP

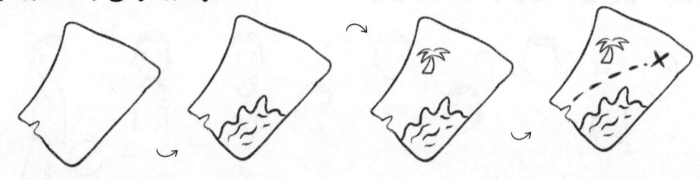

PIRATE SCARF

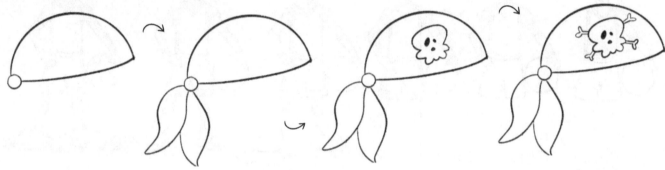

PIRATE

97

BASEBALL PLAYER

BASKETBALL HOOP AND BALL

SOCCER PLAYER

SOCCER BALL

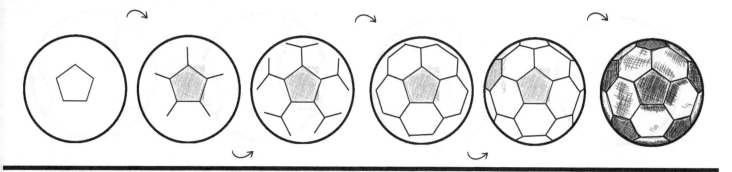

SOCCER GOAL

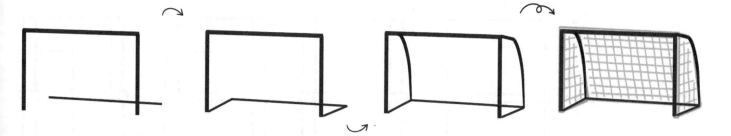

WINNER CUP

TENNIS RACKET

TENNIS BALL

TENNIS COURT

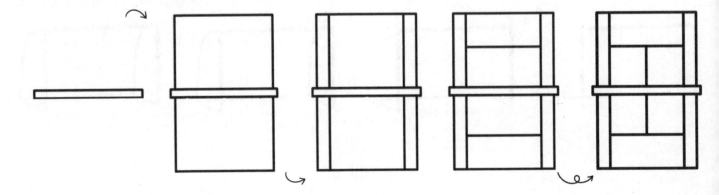

SURFBOARD

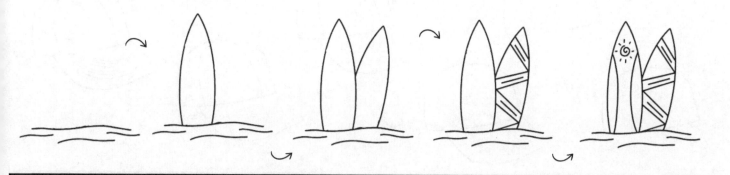

HAWAIIAN SHIRT

KITE

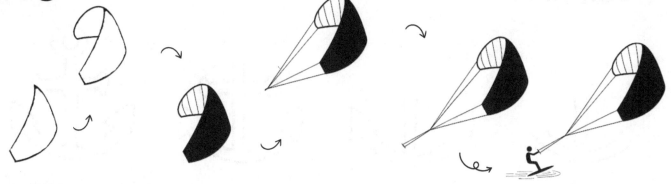

WAVE

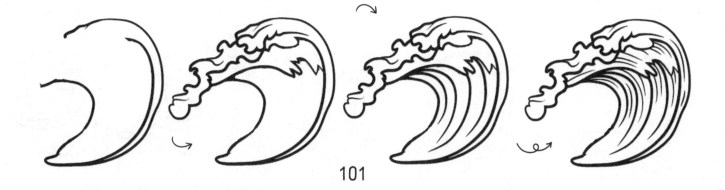

CAP

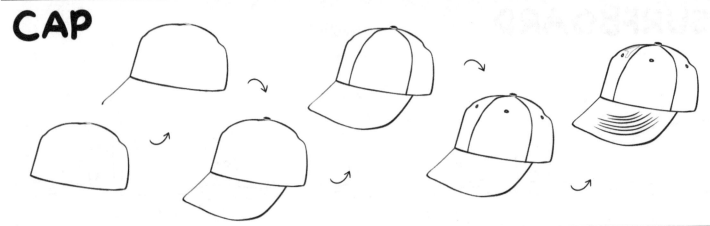

FLOATY

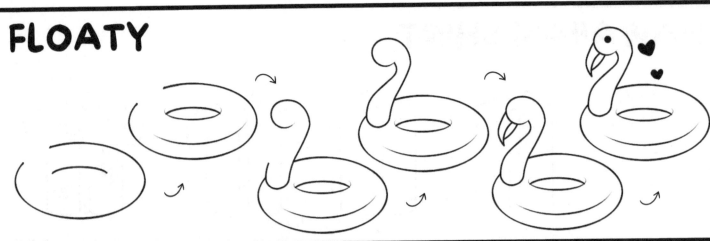

ANCHOR

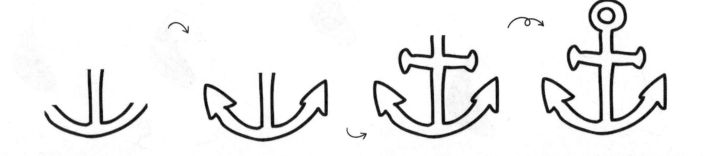

SAND BUCKET

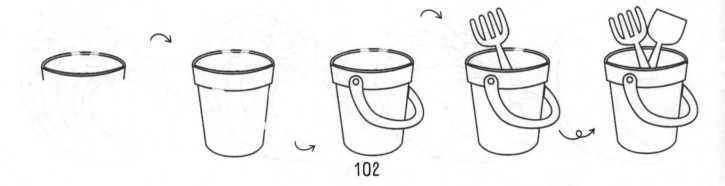

RUGBY BALL

FRISBEE

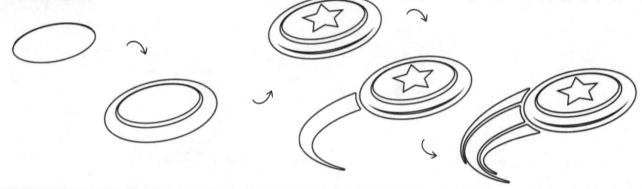

DIVING GOGGLES

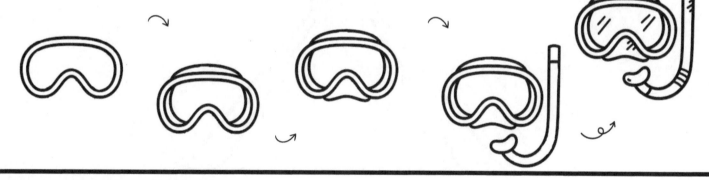

DIVING FINS

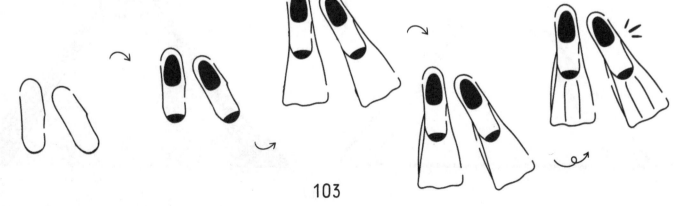

103

BOWLING PINS

BOWLING BALL

BOWLING ALLEY

PAWN CHESS PIECE

KNIGHT

ROOK CHESS PIECE

BISHOP CHESS PIECE

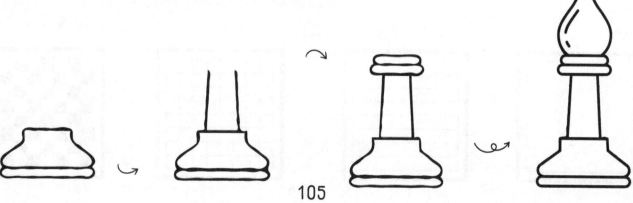

105

QUEEN CHESS PIECE

KING CHESS PIECE

CHESS CLOCK

CHESS BOARD

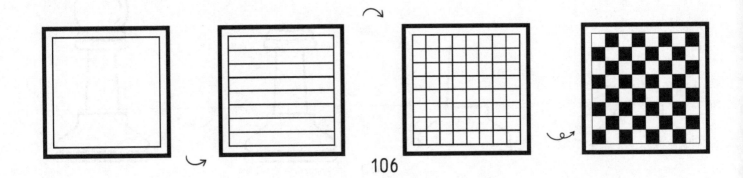

106

DICE

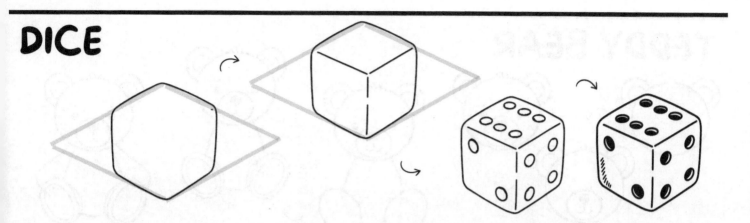

PLAYING CARDS

CHECKERS

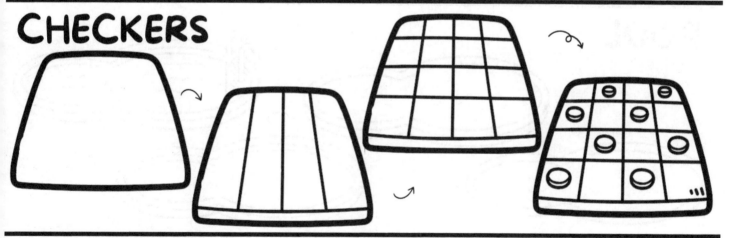

DOMINOES

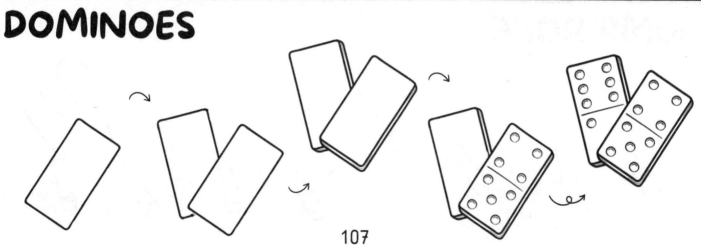

TEDDY BEAR

TRAMPOLINE

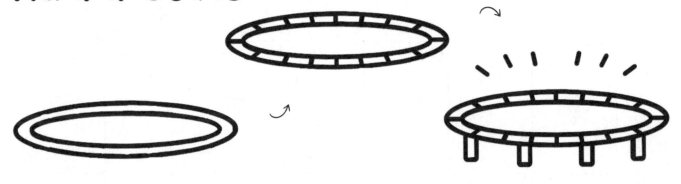

POOL

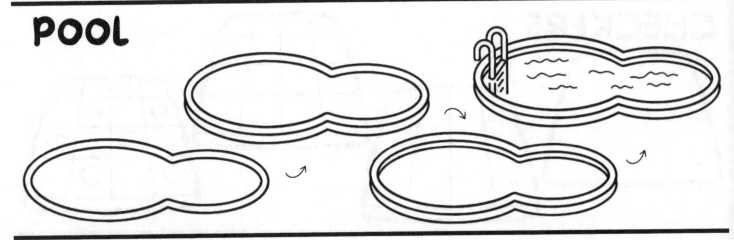

JUMP ROPE

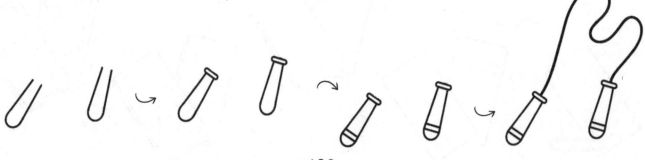

ROBOT

ROBOT WAVING

SURVEILLANCE ROBOT

ROBOTIC ARM

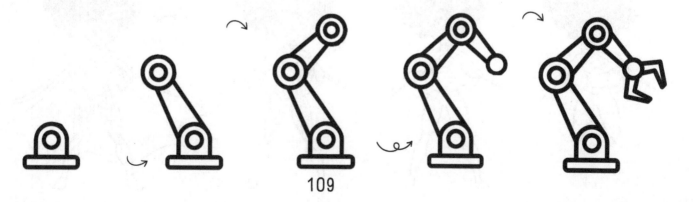

SUPERHERO MASK

SUPERHERO

Made in United States
Troutdale, OR
12/12/2024

26349101R00064